Kudos from Pat

"Comrade and brother-in-arms! . . . Your slogans are close and understandable to us."
> —Vladimir V. Zhirinovsky
> Ultranationalist candidate
> for the Russian presidency
> *Los Angeles Times*,
> February 27, 1996

"Liberty Lobby is proud to have laid the groundwork for Buchanan's candidacy and for changing the mood of the country to make that candidacy possible."
> —Vince Ryan
> Senior Editor of *Spotlight*

"Pat's general platform is absolutely verbatim with those things that we've been talking about. . . . Everything he says, it looks like I wrote it for his platform."
> —Bob Fletcher
> Former Montana militia leader

"I think that he's the best of the Republican lot."
> —David Duke
> Former Ku Klux Klan leader
> and founder of the
> National Association for the
> Advancement of White People

"Deng Xiaoping Is a Chain-Smoking Communist Dwarf"

THE SAYINGS OF PAT BUCHANAN

Edited by
S. Thomas Colfax

BALLANTINE BOOKS
NEW YORK

To the better angels of our nature.

This book is not authorized by Pat Buchanan or any member of the Buchanan campaign; neither Buchanan nor any member of his campaign has given any permission or support in connection with its publication.

http://www.randomhouse.com

Library of Congress Catalog Card Number: 96-96250

ISBN: 0-345-40783-0

Cover photo © Patsy Lynch/Retna Ltd.
Cover design by Ruth Ross
Text design by Holly Johnson

Manufactured in the United States of America

First Edition: April 1996

10 9 8 7 6 5 4 3 2 1

Introduction

Pat Buchanan's use of the English language is not particularly graceful. He uses words for their ability to cut and slash. When he writes, he is more like a Green Beret wielding a Bowie knife than a heart surgeon a scalpel. But he is effective. He almost always finds his target. And his message is clear: Politics is a blood sport between Us and Them.

Whether he is to be remembered as a populist or a demagogue is for others to judge. But what can be said today is this: No other major presidential candidate in recent American history can be measured so completely by his own words as Patrick J. Buchanan.

Buchanan's entire adult life has been taken up, in one way or another, by the business of writing and speaking words and manipulating symbols. His career has represented a steady climb to the apex of the mass media food chain: from St. Louis editorial writer to Nixon White House speechwriter to independent newspaper columnist; from radio pundit to national television personality; from communications director for Ronald Reagan to chief speechwriter and sound-bite artist for his own presidential campaign.

When Pat Buchanan goes after the media elite, he is attacking people very much like Pat Buchanan. He is a graduate of the West Point of the media elite, the Columbia School of Journalism. So Buchanan knows what he is doing when he speaks and writes; he understands the power of incendiary and divisive rhetoric in American politics. There are plenty of American politicians who don't mean what they say. Pat Buchanan is not one of them.

One of Buchanan's favorite aphorisms is that words and ideas have consequences. So he has no reason to hide from his own mountain of words, accumulated over nearly 30 years in public life. Other politicians can point to bridges or navy ships or municipal buildings named in their honor thanks to a bill pushed through Congress or the state legislature. Buchanan has a byline file.

He tacitly acknowledged as much in his 1988 autobiography, *Right from the Beginning*. One reason he decided not to make an initial run for the presidency that year, Buchanan conceded in his memoirs, was that he didn't "want to spend much of my campaign explaining the million words I had written in my controversial syndicated column of ten years . . . [or] the second million, written confidentially in earlier White House days, and secreted in the Nixon files."

Buchanan has outgrown such reticence and on the hustings now simply dismisses or ignores critics who call him to task for his past statements. But the first and second million words are still there, now joined by perhaps a third from the last eight years of writing, speaking, and baiting his foes as an agent provocateur of the Right.

Baiting is a word Buchanan might use himself to describe his rhetorical strategy. He often chastises fellow conservatives for attempting to maintain civility in debates with ideological opponents. "The times," he wrote, require that "we not only boldly enunciate our agenda for America, but expose and attack, with all the political weapons in our armory."

So it is quite fair to hold Buchanan to his words, words that have convinced many Americans that he is a racist, an anti-Semite, and a xenophobic isolationist. He can be held accountable for exploiting fear and hate, for using words that divide. He has had hundreds of opportunities to convince his readers and listeners otherwise. Instead, his accumulated words form—as Buchanan might say with nineteenth-century flourish—a bill of particulars against him.

In fact, it is his own competence at using the language that provides the most damning evidence against him. He often insists that he has been misunderstood or unfairly labeled by his critics, yet a thorough reading of his columns, speeches, and memos, and transcripts of his television appearances makes plain just how well he has learned the subtle art of pushing the envelope of socially acceptable speech. Again and again he calibrates his rhetoric, carefully pushing just far enough to inflame, but not so far that he loses his last shreds of deniability.

Charging that Israel's "Amen corner" in the United States was behind the campaign for U.S. involvement in the Persian Gulf, he listed four prominent Jews as the leading American voices supporting military action against Iraq. Yet he wrote that the war's casualties would be "American kids with names like McAllister, Murphy, Gonzales, and Leroy Brown"—not a Jewish name among them. Buchanan didn't need to draw his own conclusion. The implication was clear, despite Buchanan's later protestations: Americans would die in a far-off place to appease the Jews.

The list of Buchanan's rhetorical targets has morphed and expanded through the years, but all of his enemies have this in common: They are out-of-touch elites trying to impose their corrupt and Godless values on the common men and women of America. "They" can be feminists, Jews, blacks, homosexuals, foreigners, free-traders, atheists, abortionists, the United Nations, intellectuals, Supreme Court justices, and corporate executives. The Republican Establishment has always held a special place in Buchanan's roll of dishonor. The foundation of the Eastern Establishment (Buchanan uses capital letters promiscuously in all his writings, like any good pamphleteer) is Wall Street and old money. And Wall Street often circles back in Buchanan's rhetoric to xenophobia and Jews—most recently to Goldman, Sachs, and Robert Rubin and their backing for the Mexican bailout.

Buchanan likes to insist that his mouthy attitude is a natural outgrowth of an American Irish-Catholic boyhood, from exposure to the unbending teachings of Jesuit priests and a collective postwar American remembrance of things past that were much better than they've been since. Yet that seems to be little more than a justification for an aggrieved outlook that has much more to do with Pat Buchanan's own temperamental life than with the thinking of a broader community. The Jesuit order in the United States has a great intellectual tradition of open academic inquiry rather than intolerance; American Irish-Catholics of Buchanan's own generation identified far more with the breezy confidence and sinewy internationalism of John F. Kennedy than with the dark fears of an uncertain future that Buchanan now peddles.

Instead, look to Buchanan himself; he has built an adult life on doing with words what he did with fists growing up in a family of nine children on the affluent side of Washington. He is still the "bully boy" of Chevy Chase, Gonzaga High, and Georgetown, still the guy most eager to start a street fight with the kids from the neighboring parish or with the police who pull him over for a traffic ticket.

It was in the Nixon White House that Buchanan finally perfected the use of words rather than fists as offensive weapons, and he has since chosen the most visceral terms to dramatize his points. But if anger and code-phrases were Buchanan's only weapons, he would have long ago sunk into obscurity.

He is so good at torching opponents because of his rapier wit; he wins audiences because he amuses and entertains while he shocks. Richard Nixon once observed that Buchanan was the only extremist he knew with a sense of humor, and there are plenty of liberal Washington pundits who would vote for Buchanan as their favorite dinner companion. His stunning ability to paint vivid word pictures gives Buchanan air supremacy over his more pedestrian political foes. While stumbling public speakers like Bob Dole struggle with prepared texts, Buchanan tosses off captivating phrasings that inevitably help him define the political debate—and agenda.

But above all, Buchanan owes his political staying power to his unerring sense of what is bothering Americans—and his joyful enthusiasm for cutting to the quick of it. While other politicians dither on what can be done or said about stagnant living standards and job insecurity, Buchanan grabs the issue as his own and runs with it, all the way to proposals for walling off (figuratively) Japanese imports and walling off (literally) job-stealing Mexican immigrants. While other politicians duck and shuffle over the issue of abortion, Buchanan shouts his fervent opposition from the rooftops. He thrives on arguing the hot-button social and cultural issues that have served as the catalyst for the political awakening of fundamentalist Christians and other "movement" conservatives.

Thus, Buchanan embraces controversy as a friend, the way a guerrilla fighter embraces the jungle. So while he may lose an election, he will have his say. And he will make certain that America listens.

—S. Thomas Colfax
March 8, 1996

On Pat Buchanan and His Style

"[L]et me make a point here. The exaggerated metaphor is really the staple of American politics."

> —*Testimony before the Senate Watergate committee, quoted in* The Washington Post, *Sept. 26, 1973*

"We're winning this battle and everybody knows it. Bob Dole is starting to sound like Pat Buchanan . . . even Bill Clinton is starting to sound like Pat Buchanan."

> —*Campaign appearance, Lexington, MA, Mar. 2, 1996. Associated Press dispatch*

"[T]he truth is that Pat Buchanan was trained at the knee of Richard Milhouse Nixon."

> —*CBS News's* Nightwatch,
> *Dec. 11, 1986*

"[It's] a fair point that Pat Buchanan has a fairly sharp edge to him."

> —*PBS's* . . . talking with David
> Frost, *1992*

"Stop calling me names. Stop the invective. You know, those people up there having a hissy fit all over Washington, they can't . . . control themselves. 'The Beast is coming. It's Pat Buchanan.' . . . I'm asking the people in the Republican Party . . . take a couple of Prozacs, fellows, calm down."

—*CBS News's* Face the Nation,
Feb. 25, 1996

"They're going to come after us with everything they've got. . . . Do not wait for orders from headquarters. Mount up, everybody!"

—*Addressing supporters following his victory in the New Hampshire primary, Manchester, NH, Feb. 20, 1996. Reporter's notes*

ON WHAT THE FOUNDING FATHERS WOULD HAVE SAID IF THE KING OF ENGLAND HAD TRIED TO TAKE THE BIBLE OUT OF COLONIAL SCHOOLS

"Lock and load!"

—*Quoted in* The Washington Post,
Feb. 18, 1996

"What kind of commentator or critic would you be if you weren't controversial . . . ? So I'm rather proud that I'm controversial. People who have been in government or politics or commentary for 10 years and are totally noncontroversial haven't said anything or done anything worth paying much attention to."

—*Interview*, The Washington Times, *May 15, 1985*

"I'm a man of some controversy.
I'm enjoying every bit of it."
　　　—*Interview*, The New York Times,
　　　Mar. 25, 1986

"I was born and raised inside the
Beltway before they built the
Beltway."
　　　—*PBS's* The Challengers '96—A
　　　Washington Week in Review
　　　Special Series, *Nov. 3, 1995*

"And, yes, as president, I would insist that Cabinet and senior staff pledge never to go to work for foreign regimes. Service in Congress—and the White House—should be an honor, not an apprenticeship to a six-figure salary working in the DC rice paddies of Japan Inc."

—*Op Ed*, The Washington Post, *Oct. 30, 1995*

"There is a decided element of trepidation and panic in the Republican establishment today because they hear the hoofbeats of this revolution. . . . I represent something dramatically different in the Republican party . . . true populist conservatism. We are the real thing."

—*Campaign appearance, Dover, NH, quoted in* Los Angeles Times, *Feb. 14, 1996*

On the
"Cultural War"

"Michael [Kinsley], I don't understand you liberals. You're concerned about a little bit of smog that might get in the air and you got all kinds of federal rules and regulations but you're utterly unconcerned about the filth that pollutes the popular culture from which the whole society has to drink."

—CNN's Crossfire, *Oct. 11, 1990*

"The [Supreme] Court routinely overrules the actions of local police boards, boards of education, and state laws under which they act. The beneficiaries of the Court's protections are members of various minorities, including criminals, atheists, homosexuals, flag-burners, illegal aliens including terrorists, convicts, and pornographers."

—*Speech to the Heritage Foundation, Jan. 29, 1996*

"What recourse do we have against justices who, enthroned for life, usurp power to fasten their soppy opinions on society? . . . For four decades the Court has been on a rampage, overturning precedents, ignoring the clear intent of the Constitution, to reshape society in its own image."

—*Op Ed*, The Houston Chronicle, *Mar. 3, 1994*

ON "POLITICAL CORRECTNESS"

"Easter is displaced by Earth Day, Christmas becomes winter break, Columbus Day a day to reflect on the cultural imperialism and genocidal racism of the 'dead white males' who raped this continent while exterminating its noblest inhabitants."

—*Pat Buchanan's syndicated column, Sept. 14, 1992*

ON "STANDARDS" FOR
THE TEACHING OF HISTORY

"[H]ere is a sleepless campaign to inculcate in American youth a revulsion toward America's past. The left's long march through our institutions is complete. Secure in tenure, they are now serving up . . . a constant diet of the same poison of anti-Americanism upon which they themselves were fed."

—*Pat Buchanan's syndicated column, Nov. 6, 1994*

"Listen, Sam [Donaldson]. You may believe you're descended from monkeys. I don't believe it. . . . I think you're a creature of God. . . . I believe that God created Heaven and Earth. . . . [Parents] have a right to insist that Godless evolution not be taught to their children."

—*ABC News's* This Week with David Brinkley, *Feb. 18, 1996*

"To some Americans, the rise of the Religious Right, a decade ago, was an ominous development; to others of us, however, it was the natural, healthy reaction of a once-Christian country that has been force-fed the poisons of paganism."

> —*Pat Buchanan's autobiography,*
> Right from the Beginning

"That Confederate battle flag is, to me, a symbol of defiance, courage, bravery in the face of overwhelming odds. And I believe that everyone should stand up for their heritage. It didn't fly over slave quarters; it flew over battlefields like Chickamauga and Cold Harbor, Antietam, and Gettysburg."

—*Republican presidential candidates debate, Columbia, SC, Feb. 29, 1996. Transcript*

"The reason why we're going after welfare is because many of us believe it is socially, morally, economically, totally ruinous of everyone involved in it. It's destructive. It's dragging down our cities. It's dragging down our civilization."

—CNN's Crossfire, *Nov. 15, 1994*

"Does it make a difference that school kids in L.A., who never heard of Robert Frost, can recite the lyrics of Ice-T and 2 Live Crew? Ask the people of Koreatown."

—*Pat Buchanan's syndicated column, Sept. 14, 1992*

ON MAGIC JOHNSON, HIV, AND
THE FEDERAL AIDS POLICY

"Is government supposed to stop the spread of AIDS among athletes. . . ? How? Are we to put federal agents outside every locker room in the NBA to hand out condoms as the players head out with their groupies for a night on the town?"

— *Op Ed*, The Houston Chronicle, *Nov. 13, 1991*

"While the nation's networks will call a five-alarm news break over the threat to America's children from Alar on apples . . . where are the investigative reporters exploring the calamity wreaked upon America's young by the pied pipers of the sexual revolution?"

—*Pat Buchanan's syndicated column, June 12, 1989*

ON 2 LIVE CREW'S
OBSCENE RAP LYRICS

"Just as there's garbage that pollutes the Potomac River, there's garbage polluting our culture. We need an Environmental Protection Agency to clean it up."

—*CNN's* Crossfire, *June 8, 1990*

"My friends, there is room in America for the fighting song of the civil rights movement, 'We Shall Overcome.' And there's got to be room for 'Dixie' as well."

—*Republican presidential candidates debate, Columbia, SC, Feb. 29, 1996. Transcript*

"We cannot raise a white flag in the cultural war, for that war is about who we are. . . . Surrender this province, and we lose America."

—*Op Ed*, The Wall Street Journal, *Jan. 21, 1993*

**ON THE UNITED NATIONS
POPULATION CONFERENCE IN CAIRO**

"Once America stood for freedom, liberty, and a Judeo-Christian moral order. Tomorrow in Cairo, the U.S. delegation will offer the world's poor IUDs, suction pumps, condoms, and Norplant."

—*Op Ed,* The Denver Post, *Sept. 4, 1994*

On Homosexuality

"Someone's values are going to prevail. Why not ours? Whose country is it, anyway? Whose moral code says we may interfere with a man's right to be a practicing bigot, but must respect and protect his right to be a practicing sodomite?"

—*Pat Buchanan's autobiography,*
Right from the Beginning

"Compassion for the victims of this dread disease [AIDS] does not relieve us of the obligation to speak the truth: Promiscuous sodomy—unnatural, unsanitary sexual relations between males, which every great religion teaches is immoral—is the cause of AIDS. Anal sex between consenting adults is spreading the virus from one homosexual to another, thence into the needles of addicts and the blood supply of hemophiliacs."

—*Pat Buchanan's autobiography,*
Right from the Beginning

"Gay rights militants are the aggressors in our cultural war. Neither Jesse Helms nor John Cardinal O'Connor goes gay-bashing, but homosexuals annually parade naked in front of St. Patrick's Cathedral, perform lewd acts on the parade route, disrupt Sunday masses and vandalize churches."

—Pat Buchanan's syndicated column, Sept. 15, 1994

"The Hensons [a lesbian couple in Ovett, MI] are provocateurs. Their camp is as offensive to Ovett as a brothel or a nudist camp. Steeped in moral arrogance, these women want to defecate on the values of a traditional community without suffering any social sanction from the people they are offending."

—*Op Ed*, San Francisco Examiner, *Mar. 18, 1994*

"Americans are a tolerant people. But a majority believes that sexual practices of gays, whether a result of nature or nurture, are morally wrong and medically ruinous. . . . To force [acceptance of the gay lifestyle] on us is like forcing Christians to burn incense to the emperor."

—*Pat Buchanan's syndicated column, Sept. 20, 1992*

"I doubt if I would appoint someone who was an out-of-the-closet homosexual . . . to a high appointive position in the Buchanan administration."

"[H]omosexuals, even though it's obviously a very powerful impulse, have the capacity not to engage in those acts. They have free will."

—*NBC News's* Meet the Press,
Feb. 11, 1996

**ON LESBIAN ROBERTA
ACHTENBERG'S CONFIRMATION BY
THE SENATE FOR A POST IN THE
CLINTON ADMINISTRATION**

"[Achtenberg's] confirmation is a statement that the old Judeo-Christian tenets of behavior are out and the moral tenets of a post-Christian humanism are in. The new standard: All consensual sexual activity is now morally equal and morally good."

—*Pat Buchanan's syndicated
column, June 2, 1993*

"[H]omosexuals have declared war upon nature and nature is exacting an awful retribution. I believe that homosexuality, like other vices, is an assault upon the nature of the individual as God made him."

> —*CBS News's* Face the Nation,
> *Mar. 26, 1995*

ON THE GAYS IN THE MILITARY CONTROVERSY

"Even Bill and Hillary must be wishing that the love-that-dare-not-speak-its-name would shut up for a while."

> —*Pat Buchanan's syndicated column, Feb. 24, 1993*

On Jewish Issues

"The Congress of the United States is Israeli-occupied territory. What I meant by that is the most powerful lobby in Washington which Congress can't stand up to, one of the most powerful, is certainly the pro-Israeli lobby. It has gotten its way in this town year in and year out."
> —The MacNeil/Lehrer NewsHour,
> *December 13, 1991*

"Oh, for heaven's sakes! Listen, we have Jewish supporters. . . . We've got rabbis on the board of our campaign. We've had Jewish friends our whole lives."

—*Responding to the question of whether he is anti-Semitic, radio interview, Manchester, NH, Feb. 16, 1996. Reported in* The New York Times, *Feb. 17, 1996*

ON THE HOLOCAUST AND THE JUSTICE DEPARTMENT OFFICE OF SPECIAL INVESTIGATIONS, WHICH HUNTS ACCUSED NAZI WAR CRIMINALS

"You've got a great atrocity that occurred 35, 45 years ago, okay? Why continue to invest . . . put millions of dollars into investigating that? I mean, why keep a special office to investigate Nazi war crimes?"

—*Television interview with Allan Ryan, Jr., then director of the Office of Special Investigations, 1982. Quoted in* New York Daily News, *Apr. 10, 1985*

"There are only two groups that are beating the drums for war in the Middle East and that is the Israeli Defense Ministry and its 'Amen' corner in the United States."

— The McLaughlin Group,
   Aug. 24, 1990

ON BEING LABELED AN ANTI-SEMITE

BY NEW YORK TIMES COLUMNIST

ABE ROSENTHAL

"Well, there goes the B'nai B'rith Man of the Year Award."

— *Pat Buchanan's syndicated column, Sept. 21, 1990*

"Anti-Semitic . . . is a term used by a very powerful special interest in America to demonize and destroy the reputation of men who stand up and disagree . . . with their agenda. Now, Pat Buchanan disagrees with the agenda of . . . the Israel lobby."

> —*PBS's* . . . talking with David Frost, *1992*

On Women

"Female militants are more of an object of ridicule and a pain in the butt than the black chauvinists."

"The Butch Brigade will be after Julie [Nixon] to come off one hundred percent for the movement."

> —*Description of the feminist movement in White House memo to H. R. Haldeman about how Julie Nixon should present herself to the public, Sept. 20, 1971*

"[F]eminists insist that 25-year-old women are as capable as men of flying combat missions. They can handle the terror of battle but need federal protection against office pigs and fanny patters."

— *Op Ed*, The Houston Chronicle, Oct. 11, 1991

ON WOMEN AT THE CITADEL
ALL-MALE MILITARY ACADEMY

"The Citadel has been breached. . . . How can it be a victory for diversity to force [The Citadel] to become like every other school?"

— *Pat Buchanan's syndicated column, Jan. 26, 1994*

On Abortion

"For those who believe in the sanctity of all human life, the abortuaries of the West are the Free World terminals for the trains that left earlier this century for destinations like Vorkuta and Kolyma, Treblinka and Auschwitz, killing fields founded on the Orwellian principle that while all human beings are equal, some are more equal than others."

—*Pat Buchanan's autobiography,*
Right from the Beginning

"I will appoint the justices that will overturn that abomination called *Roe v. Wade*."

—*Appearance before Christian Coalition rally, Manchester, NH, Feb. 16, 1996. Quoted in* The Washington Post, *Feb. 18, 1996*

"I believe that the unborn child is made in the image and likeness of God and that there is never a justification for its deliberate destruction."

"I believe the 34 million abortions we've had in this country is the greatest atrocity and travesty and horror in our country's history."

—Republican presidential candidates debate, Columbia, SC, Feb. 29, 1996. Transcript

On Racial Issues

———

"[I]t seems to me that a lot
of what we are doing in terms
of integration of blacks and
whites . . . is less likely to result
in accommodation than it is
in perpetual friction—as the
incapable are played consciously
by government side by side with
the capable."

—*White House memo,*
Aug. 26, 1971

"Here [in Washington, DC], despite a generous welfare system, its beneficiaries are resentful. Here, though almost all positions of power are held by minorities (mayor, city council, school board, police, fire department) and preferential treatment is routine in hiring—still, talk radio and the press are filled with venomous tirades about white 'racism.' "

—Pat Buchanan's syndicated column, Apr. 4, 1994

"The Republican philosophy of limited government is seen as colliding head-on with black America's perceived interest in the expansion of Federal power. The party's . . . hope . . . rests upon cultivation of unfashionable minorities—Irish, Italians . . . Czechs . . . Jews and, yes, WASPs—victimized by the very discriminatory policies from which black America benefits."

—*Op Ed*, The New York Times, *Apr. 5, 1977*

"The race of the defendant, not the weight of the evidence, is becoming the prime consideration in racially tinged trials."

—*Op Ed*, The Houston Chronicle,
Mar. 5, 1993

"Let us hope that the L.A. riot, where aliens joined homegrown thugs to maim, loot, and lynch, is not America's future."

—*Op Ed*, Pittsburgh Post-Gazette,
July 12, 1993

ON THE POLICE BEATING
OF RODNEY KING

"[T]he ref should have stepped in and stopped this thing, but as a cop, can't you understand that— you know, how these guys are feeling after this chase is all over?"

— *CNN's* Crossfire, *Mar. 6, 1991*

ON THE O. J. SIMPSON VERDICT

"[It] offended Americans because it appeared to be a moral outrage. An individual whom . . . [an] Everest of evidence showed was guilty, has walked free to a party. There's been jubilation and exaltation . . . and I think that moral outrage is justified."

—*CBS News's* Face the Nation,
Oct. 8, 1995

ON MARTIN LUTHER KING JR.

"If the man has . . . character
flaws that get men kicked out of
presidential races, why should you
ask American kids to hold him up
as a role model and why should
the rest of us be required to set
aside a day to honor him?"
—*CNN's* Crossfire, *Nov. 12, 1990*

"Perhaps some other use of Alcatraz can be found—if we can get the Redskins off."

> —*Memo to Chuck Colson, Sept. 7, 1971*

ON AFFIRMATIVE ACTION

"America should be listening for drums along the racial frontier."

> —*Pat Buchanan's syndicated column, Jan. 23, 1995*

"Quiet down, children, or I'll take your . . . grants away."

"What we have here is the revolt of the overprivileged."

> —*Mocking replies to protesters who accused him of racism and anti-Semitism, Lexington, MA, Mar. 2, 1996. Associated Press dispatch*

"The reason 150 million Africans are suffering malnutrition and hunger is not a lack of U.S. aid; it is the presence across that continent of some of the most incompetent and malodorous kakistocracies on earth."

—*Op Ed*, The Philadelphia
Inquirer, *Nov. 21, 1984*

On Immigration

"I think God made all people good, but if we had to take a million immigrants in, say, Zulus, next year, or Englishmen and put them in Virginia, what group would be easier to assimilate and would cause less problems for the people of Virginia?"

— *ABC News's* This Week with
David Brinkley, *Dec. 8, 1991*

"I'll term-limit these federal judges, declare a time out on new immigration, secure America's borders, and insist on one language—English—for all Americans."

> *—Campaign advertisement, released Feb. 27, 1996*

"I'll build that security fence, and we'll close it! And we'll say, 'Listen, Jose, you're not coming in this time!' "

> *—Campaign rally, Waterloo, IA, January 1996*

"Should we be concerned that
Americans of European descent
will be a minority in . . . the entire
U.S. by the middle of the next
century? . . . I want to save and
preserve the country I grew up
in and I'll be honest. I don't want
to live in the Brazil of North
America."

     —*CNN's* Crossfire, *Sept. 13, 1991*

"America is our country. Americans—
no one else—should decide who
comes and who does not. And
what, after all, is a country, if not
a separate people with their own
laws, language, history, culture,
and identity? . . . Anyone up for
taking America back?"

> —*Pat Buchanan's syndicated
> column, Dec. 19, 1994*

On Foreign Policy

"Why not legislate U.S. withdrawal from all these blood-sucking multinational banks, like the World Bank, phase out foreign aid, and give the $15 billion back to taxpayers?"

> —*Op Ed*, The Denver Post,
> *Nov. 20, 1994*

"The world is not a country club of chums. It is the NFL, where the fellows across the line will do what they have to to take away that Super Bowl ring we've been wearing all these years. Let's put on our game face."

—*Pat Buchanan's syndicated column, Jan. 16, 1995*

ON TRADE

"All four presidents on Mt. Rushmore were protectionists."
—*Pat Buchanan's syndicated column, Dec. 5, 1994*

"What we need is a president of the United States who's gonna tell the Europeans, 'Listen, fellas, you're going to play fair or we're going to play rough.' "
—*Campaign appearance, Creston, IA, Feb. 8, 1996. Reporter's notes*

ON MEXICO

"With NAFTA, the United States
made an incompetent, corrupt,
and now bankrupt regime a full
partner. Now U.S. citizens are going
to have to underwrite that partner's
gambling debts. And, oh yeah, I
almost forgot: I told you so."

—*Pat Buchanan's syndicated
column, Jan. 3, 1995*

ON THE MEXICAN BAILOUT

"Newly installed President Ernesto Zedillo said he needed the cash to pay off bonds held by Citibank and Goldman Sachs, lest the New World Order come crashing down around the ears of its panicked acolytes. We shall never see the money again. Our grandchildren will pay it off."

—*Op Ed,* The Sacramento Bee,
Sept. 1, 1995

ON WHY HE OPPOSES
SANCTIONS AGAINST APARTHEID
IN SOUTH AFRICA

"When the Xhosa and Zulu peoples, confined in their segregated townships, are also jobless and hungry, will we all sleep better in Chevy Chase and Georgetown?"

—*Op Ed*, The New York Times, *Sept. 18, 1986*

On Democrats

"Homosexuals in the barracks, Boy-Scout bashing, condoms in the classroom, racial balance in public housing, Catholic-baiting, Christian-bashing, inviting HIV-positives to a gay jamboree in New York, defending nutcake art—why did they do it?"

—Pat Buchanan's syndicated column, June 30, 1994

"Bill and Hillary are going to end up as the Jim and Tammy Faye Bakker of American liberalism. No denying it, there is glee among the peasantry . . . the glee of people who have seen their adversaries' pretensions to moral superiority exposed as hypocrisy and fraud."

—*Pat Buchanan's syndicated column, Mar. 28, 1994*

"Of all the disabling disorders of the Democratic Left, its own stuffy superiority complex is perhaps the most serious."

—*Pat Buchanan's syndicated column, Aug. 15, 1991*

"Democrats are more ruthless and purposeful. For them this is not a game. It is what life is all about."

—*Op Ed*, San Francisco Examiner, *Nov. 29, 1993*

**ON THE 1992 DEMOCRATIC
NATIONAL CONVENTION**

"[T]hat giant masquerade ball up at Madison Square Garden—where 20,000 radicals and liberals came dressed up as moderates and centrists in the greatest single exhibition of cross-dressing in American political history."

> —*Floor remarks, 1992 Republican National Convention, Houston, TX*

"As the [1972] campaign progresses, we should increasingly portray McGovern as the pet radical of Eastern Liberalism, the darling of the *New York Times*, the hero of the Berkeley Hill Jet Set; Mr. Radical Chic."

> —*"Assault Strategy" memo to President Nixon for planning the 1972 campaign, June 8, 1972*

"Hillary [Clinton] could rise at Wellesley's graduation and deliver an arrogant little speech about the moral superiority of her generation, and be burbled over for it in the national press, the way rich and indulgent parents burble over a favorite infant pooping on the living room rug."

—*Pat Buchanan's syndicated column, Dec. 30, 1994*

"When his wife, eight months pregnant, lost a child in '56, JFK went off boating with a passel of bimbos in the Mediterranean. . . . Neither JFK nor [Martin Luther] King could have survived that Iroquois gauntlet Judge [Clarence] Thomas was forced to run."

—Pat Buchanan's syndicated column, Oct. 18, 1991

On Republicans

"By leaning now left, now right, Mr. Bush has excited no one, but then, he has fatally antagonized no one, which, in the galaxy of the moderate Republican, is, apparently, the best of all possible worlds."

—*Pat Buchanan's syndicated column, Nov. 6, 1989*

ON COLIN POWELL

"No, I don't think [his race is a problem]. He's called himself a Rockefeller Republican, and the original Nelson Rockefeller was as white as the eleventh Earl of Sandwich."

> —*ABC News's* This Week with David Brinkley, *Oct. 29, 1995*

"He's a good soldier, but he's Bill Clinton on the social issues."

> —*Remarks at airport rally, Florence, SC, Mar. 1, 1996. Quoted in* The New York Times, *Mar. 2, 1996*

ON DAVID DUKE

"Take a hard look at Duke's portfolio of winning issues, and expropriate those not in conflict with GOP principles. . . . Duke's message comes across as middle class, meritocratic, populist, and nationalist."

—*Op Ed,* The Houston Chronicle, *Oct. 24, 1991*

ON RICHARD NIXON

"[H]is victories over the
Establishment . . . earned him
the eternal enmity of the
Establishment. And when Richard
Nixon stumbled and fell, they
would all be in on the kill."

> —*Pat Buchanan's syndicated
> column, Apr. 27, 1994*

"Lionel Trilling in a room with
the Old Man [Nixon] . . . would
be about as much in place as the
President amidst Sly and the
Family Stone."

> —*White House memo in response to
> a suggestion that Nixon appear
> with prominent intellectuals,
> Sept. 17, 1971*

"I have never been convinced that Richard Nixon, Good Guy, is our long suit; to me we are simply not going to charm the American people; we are not going to win it on 'style' and we ought to forget playing ball in the Kennedys' court."

—*White House memo, Sept. 17, 1971*

ON BOB DOLE

"Mr. NAFTA. Mr. GATT. Mr. Mexico bailout."

"My friend Bob Dole is an Archer Daniels Midland Republican. He has been hauling water for the same corporate interests that he's condemning this morning."

—Campaign appearance, Dover, NH, Feb. 14, 1996. Reporter's notes

On the Media

"If the sexual revolution has been a medical disaster, socially it has been a catastrophe. . . . Why do the media not report and explore the tragic results of the sexual revolution? Because many are collaborators."

—*Pat Buchanan's syndicated column, June 13, 1989*

"I think that in the minds of many, the press is being seen less and less as a neutral observer in the impeachment enterprise and more and more as participants, or even collaborators."

—*White House press conference,*
June 19, 1974

"If a powerful, hostile institution, like the national press in Nixon's era, is implacable, unappeasable, one might as well reap the benefit of that hostility, by inviting the support of those who have come to distrust or despise that institution."

> —*Pat Buchanan's syndicated column, Mar. 26, 1988*

On Other Issues

"Were flogging to be introduced
in New York, for spray-painting
subway cars, how long would it be
before those cars were immaculate
and safe again?"

—*Pat Buchanan's syndicated
column, Apr. 11, 1994*

ON BURNING THE AMERICAN FLAG

"It's like going up and saying,
'Your mother is a tramp.' "

—*CNN's Crossfire, June 11, 1990*

ON ADOLF HITLER

"[Hitler's] genius was an intuitive sense of . . . the weakness masquerading as morality that was in the hearts of the statesmen who stood in his path."

"Though Hitler was indeed racist and anti-Semitic to the core . . . he was also an individual of great courage, a soldier's soldier in the Great War, a leader."

—*Pat Buchanan's syndicated column, Aug. 25, 1977*

ON RELATIONS WITH CAPITOL HILL

"Congress is a bully and a coward. . . . Congress will bawl, bitch, and bellyache to the press and do nothing. Rely upon it."

—*Pat Buchanan's syndicated column, Mar. 22, 1988*

ON ELECTIONS

"Defeat has its lessons as well as victory."

—*Op Ed,* The Washington Post, *Nov. 10, 1974*

ON GUNS

"Isn't the problem rather than dangerous guns really lousy people? I mean, we have much easier gun laws . . . in Virginia and we don't have anything like the massacres and murders that you're conducting here in Washington, DC."

—*CNN's* Crossfire, *Dec. 19, 1990*

ON DR. ALFRED KINSEY
AND HIS SEX RESEARCH

"Al Kinsey was a charlatan, a fraud, and possibly a serial child molester. . . . There are only two ways Kinsey could have confirmed the reactions of those children. One is to have collaborated in molesting them. The second is to have relied on the testimony of pedophiles."

—*Pat Buchanan's syndicated column, Sept. 9, 1993*

"We don't make apologies."
—CBS This Morning, *Feb. 20, 1996*